Let's Get Active™

LET'S LEARN
MARTIAL ARTS

Shane McFee

PowerKiDS
press™
New York

Published in 2008 by The Rosen Publishing Group, Inc.
29 East 21st Street, New York, NY 10010

First Edition

Editors: Nicole Pristash and Jennifer Way
Book Design: Greg Tucker
Photo Researcher: Nicole Pristash

Photo Credits: Cover © Laura Ciapponi/Getty Images; pp. 5, 21 © Getty Images; pp. 7, 9, 13, 15 Shutterstock.com; p. 11 © Anna Crawford/Getty Images; p. 17 by Lance Cpl. Patrick M. Johnson-Cambell; p. 19 © Tony Hopewell/Getty Images.

Library of Congress Cataloging-in-Publication Data

McFee, Shane.
    Let's learn martial arts / by Shane McFee. — 1st ed.
        p. cm. — (Let's get active)
    Includes index.
    ISBN 978-1-4042-4196-1 (library binding)
    1. Martial arts—Juvenile literature. I. Title.
    GV1101.35.M34 2008
    796.8—dc22

                                          2007034697

Manufactured in the United States of America

Contents

Martial Arts

Do you or does someone you know practice martial arts? Martial arts are some of the most popular sports in the world. People from many different countries practice martial arts. A martial art is a system of fighting that uses special skills and moves. There are many different forms, such as karate, tae kwon do, and judo.

Martial arts are used mostly for **self-defense** and sport. They can require years of study and practice. Martial arts are also a great form of exercise.

Martial arts can teach you how to keep yourself safe. They are also a great way to feel good about yourself!

What Are Martial Arts?

Most martial arts come from the Eastern part of the world. The most popular forms began in Asia. They are still practiced there by millions of people. The object of most martial arts is to beat your **opponent**. Some forms, however, teach **meditation**. Meditation can be very healthy. Some people practice martial arts just to stay healthy, and they do not **compete** in competitions.

Martial arts are like a lot of other activities. For example, boxing is based on martial arts. Martial arts and dance are alike, too. They both require the body to move in special ways.

These kids are doing a Brazilian dance that mixes martial arts and dance moves. It is called capoeira (kah-puh-WAY-ruh).

Karate

Karate (kuh-RAH-tee) is an old martial art. It is a skill that began on the Japanese island of Okinawa. Karate began when the Japanese mixed their own moves with skills they learned from the Chinese.

Karate means "hand" in an old Chinese language. It also sounds like the Japanese word for "empty hand." There are no **weapons** used in karate. Instead, when practicing karate, you strike with your hands. Karate also uses kicks and throws. Throws are just what you think they are. Trying to throw your opponent is a throw.

These two boys are practicing together. This is called sparring. Sparring will help the boys get better at karate.

Tae Kwon Do

Tae kwon do (TY KWAHN DOH) is one of the most popular martial arts in the world. It is the main sport of South Korea. "Tae kwon do" means "foot hand way." Koreans first practiced it to make themselves fast and **agile**.

Tae kwon do uses more kicks than most martial arts. The first people to practice tae kwon do believed that the leg is the strongest part of the body. Because of this, they invented a martial art that used mainly the legs. People who do tae kwon do also practice breaking wooden boards. You have likely seen this on television.

Many tae kwon do martial artists perform kicks while in the air. This boy is doing a flying roundhouse kick!

Judo

Judo (JOO-doh) is a Japanese martial art. It means "the gentle way." Judo is called gentle, or soft, because it does not use as many hits or kicks as karate and tae kwon do.

The object of judo is to gain control over your opponent. When practicing judo, you try to force your opponent onto his back. This is called pinning. If you can pin your opponent, you are in control. Balance is very important in judo as well. If you lose your balance, you are easy to pin.

One of the main goals of judo is to throw your opponent to the floor. Once he is on the floor, he is easier to pin.

Learning Martial Arts

Many people practice martial arts in a dojo. *Dojo* means "place of the way" in Japanese. Most dojos are like gyms. They have teachers who train students.

Many people who practice martial arts wear belts. You can tell how skilled a person is by the color of the belt he wears. Most beginners start with a white belt. As they learn new and different skills, they get a new belt with a different color. A black belt means a person has learned all the basic martial arts skills. This person can now go on and learn even harder skills.

The boy on the left has earned a red belt. This means he has learned more skills than the other boy, who is wearing a blue belt.

Martial Arts on the Job

Many American, British, and Canadian **soldiers** practice martial arts moves for self-defense. Most of these moves, like holds, are used to **disarm** opponents. Soldiers also learn what parts of the body to attack. Some of these body parts are called pressure points. Striking a pressure point can cause lots of pain without causing lasting harm.

Police officers also use martial arts movements when they **restrain** people. These moves are useful when the police need to control someone without hurting them. Learning martial arts can save lives.

These men are members of the Marine Corps. Their martial arts skills will help them fight enemies in battle.

Honor

People who practice martial arts learn more than just kicks and moves. They learn the value of sportsmanship. Sportsmanship means never **cheating**. It also means not getting upset if you lose and not showing off if you win.

Martial artists also value honor. Honor means always treating your opponent with respect. Most martial arts practices and competitions begin with the opponents bowing to each other. This is a sign of respect. Many karate students make a promise never to use karate to hurt people. This is also a sign of honor. People who practice martial arts know that honor and sportsmanship go together.

These two martial artists are bowing to each other before they practice. They are showing respect for one another.

Meet Steven Lopez

Steven Lopez is one of the greatest tae kwon do martial artists of all time. He is from Sugar Land, Texas. Lopez began practicing tae kwon do when he was only five years old. Today, he is the tae kwon do world **champion**. Lopez won the gold **medal** for the U.S. team at the Summer Olympics in 2000 and 2004.

Tae kwon do skills run in Lopez's family. His brother Mark and his sister Diana are also famous tae kwon do artists. Their oldest brother Jean is their teacher. Lopez's dream is that he and his brothers and sisters could compete on the same Olympic team!

As of 2007, Steven Lopez (left) has won more medals than any other tae kwon do martial artist in history!

Let's Get Active!

Do you want to practice martial arts? The first thing you can do is find a good school or teacher. Ask your parents to help you. You can check the phone book to see if there is a dojo near you. You can also learn more about martial arts and dojos on the Internet or at a library.

Practicing a martial art can help you accomplish things that you never thought were possible. Did you ever think you could break a board with your hands? With the help of a martial arts teacher, maybe you can!

Glossary

agile (A-jul) Able to move easily and beautifully.

champion (CHAM-pee-un) Someone who is the best or a winner at something.

cheating (CHEET-ing) Acting unfairly in order to win a game.

compete (kum-PEET) To oppose another in a game or test.

disarm (dis-AHRM) To remove a weapon from an opponent's hand.

medal (MEH-dul) A small, round object that is given as a prize or honor.

meditation (meh-dih-TAY-shun) The act of keeping one's thoughts on something.

opponent (uh-POH-nent) A person or a group that is against another.

restrain (rih-STRAYN) To hold someone or to stop someone from moving.

self-defense (self-dih-FENS) Guarding oneself from a fight.

soldiers (SOHL-jurz) People who are in an army.

weapons (WEH-punz) Objects or tools used to hurt or kill.

Index

Web Sites

Due to the changing nature of Internet links, PowerKids Press has developed an online list of Web sites related to the subject of this book. This site is updated regularly. Please use this link to access the list:
www.powerkidslinks.com/lga/mart/